LEVON HELM

JASON MORRIS

ugly duckling presse
brooklyn, 2018

ISBN 978-1-946433-11-4
First Edition, First Printing, 2018
1000 copies

Ugly Duckling Presse
The Old American Can Factory
232 Third Street #E-303
Brooklyn, NY 11215
www.uglyducklingpresse.org

Distributed in the USA by SPD/Small Press Distribution

Design and typesetting by Sarah Lawson
Cover art by J Grabowski
The type is Perpetua with titles in Requiem
Offset printing and binding by McNaughton & Gunn

This book was published with the support of the
New York State Council on the Arts.

NYSCA
New York State Council on the Arts

Contents

APHASIA

Thin newsprint, a little ripped
on which you wrote
LANGUAGE IS THE THRONE OF THE OTHER
I was able to get inside of the building
but I'd lost the piece of paper
on which I'd written all of the codes
outside the day's grays and greens
a fluid human movement we slipped into
I grew confused & trusted in you
your honesty formed the spine
of my mysterious neutrality
There are no vipers in this poem
we continued walking until
we were way out in the cuts, collecting
wildflowers by the highway abutment
I'd gotten stuff for sandwiches
you were talking about feeling like
you should want something beyond
even poetry or love, can you
name what that something is
wanting to not want is more accurately
religious, how now we're where we were

POLARIS

Orange juice bagel
Cream cheese & lox
Iced coffee cigarettes & newspaper
Which is expanding into
Who knows what
The bus I cheated
Death to ride
Poetry is a force
Unpublished writing assumes
Very fucking despacio
& full of graffiti
w/ NO MISSPELLINGS EVER
Heavy plates
Elegantly lowered
On centered hooks to cover
Street construction
My credit is birdshit, a paw
The fog forms as its long arm
Cuddles the city slowly
Lighting certain curtained
Windows below the careful
Exception nightfall continues to make
Laconic as a rock
Escarpment, drinking
What Coolidge calls approach beers
Close to Fair on Mission
A van goes by w TIME on the side
Tourniquet
Each stands in dubious reprieve

I like to weigh my options
Another humanoid division
Wand'ring across my eye
Where were we now
Cacti & stars

THE HISTORY OF THE EARTH

As it heads out toward the margin, clouds—
East. Range of motion: to be
any open window sound comes through. Violins
on a chinatown alley, Saturday afternoon
    by a flowershop—

"An attempt to imagine a universe in which
action is atomic leads the mind into a state
of hopeless confusion"
                    —James Jeans,
    "Report on Radiation & the Quantum-
Theory" (London: The Electrician
Publishing Co., 1914)

        trying to remember
          the word
            'samsara'
     all I could think of
        was 'mergatroid'

N.B. How many of the finest thoughts
one has here on earth, as on awakening
to rain, or when there appears a removal
of the mind from itself, as in a trance:
what impossible number of these
remain unwritten, fallen prey to mere
stylistic decisions of wording?
                    "This is not
    what I paid a lot of money to hear"

A HASH

of thought, ok
at day's end, my
impatience now
suddenly absolute
the record is over
Zugzwang. I get

up & flip it, needle screeches lost ugly handwritten
locomotive marginalia & downwardly now
suddenly mobile. The whole table folds, re-
antes. Next round the sumptuous moment she asks
to slower go, I read over the course of several

such days: how dissolute
do you wanna get? The history of a lilypad
a matter of earliest tadpole eyes. Every letter

a drawn sound
nears the twilit calyx
like a pyramid of packed
sand seen arising distantly over
sand reddening at day's end. Beautifully
to dull all horizons, the said. You can call it
a criminal world—

Fahey pawning his guitar
pumping gas

in the head they're
peacock feathers, oil stains: traces
of earth's names in the rain as the asphalt
covering it dries—Argos' hundreds of eyes

ERIS

A lot of glare on the freeways of the tri-state area
I'd like a handful of cold, fresh raspberries to eat
Some people stare on the streets openly, or look at their feet
I'd spike my own drink with pills in this heat
You make me have a feeling, often I don't have one
My hopes get dashed, I feel I belong nowhere
My sneakers are untied, all the guys in the offices are leaving for lunch
I cut sails from financial districts, if cities are brains they would be
The brain damaged parts of them, everyone isolated on phones
I hunch over the poem like it's you are my enemy, everything
I test by lines, write down things I recall feeling other times
This is the product of a lot of people talking
Everything seems to rhyme initially then gets messed up
That's right of course I remember you now

EVENING IN HAYWARD

Easy having a meeting on the ridge
dreamily exchanging indispensable
information that simply comes and goes

How do we get the check here, Leo?

That the heart remains impelled to hitch a ride
on the garbage truck of language
basking even as it is in Hawthornian moonlight
Across from which appear these almost
daylit phenomena, slumped and shunted
from which one then faithfully records

Triple bar
Triple mind
Triple cherry

Coming on as sumptuous
as evening in Oakland, or a darkness over towns
farther east. You only get to read it
for the first time once: slow down. Diagonal
pollen, along with the announcer's voice
A river. It has to do with but not exactly

alchemy, simple depiction of light & shade—

A nest in the backyard has finally hatched
& now I see how flight is finished
before it's begun: as a sort of desultory
serial hopping, a starting & stopping
along with lots of inchoate early song

RIVER

In a gray van w/ no heat
full of smoke, the windows
barely cracked against the cold
rolling steady
progression of miles
one North American city
to the next
Fluid sluice
of war & commerce
Ringing w/ good jazz
the ambition to write a poem
    enough
to frighten off raw wonder
& left coughing, eyes
tear up
unable to explain even
ports, parts, a defense against
real witchcraft
    & also those that hunt them
taking flight into the
flat, full light
Of a midwestern winter afternoon
I didn't know the crystallizing air
one's pulled outward toward
bright limpid reckless & dry
might so lightly wear it:
Wherein inheres a wild similarity
between all of the day's parts
    particulars

I meant to
name specifically
the place I initially pushed
& stole thereby (unknowingly)
admittance. Fell.
It goes on for so many pages
chronological but disjointed
each its own episode & jagged
around the edges. Painted
quickly & quickly set
into a set, ie., one in a series. Carrying
     them
so slowly
but never gone—
away—I want an unfamiliar thought
more obscenity
(off stage life)
If the petals are always
dropping into
the river & the river is
always there, always
moving as if under
flowering boughs
carrying clearly along
this almost weightless
freight—little
petals mind holds afloat
I think of the sweat
back of her neck

watching her shouting
singing scatting
in the rose colored room
not that long ago
a close room w/ low light
set up so as to be
conducive to the music. I want
to name the place & song—in
the van the music's lost
a blast or ribbon
Many birds
in sudden flight. Static
smoke & snow—signal
What is the gesture
What is the color
What is the time or place
Denying
the identity of indiscernibles
Just zoning out / zeroing in on
the horizon
Look at me I can't even talk
& walk away from therein
its perpetual & beautifully
obscene continuance

UDFj-39546284   El Gordo   Pandora's Cluster   Silver Coin

Barnard's   Red Spider   Ghost of Jupiter   Eye of God

Dog Star   Sun   Moon

1958 Vanguard 1   South Pole

Plaza Mayor   Plaza de Los Mariachis   Tiburon Island

Los Angeles County Museum of Art   China One Express King City, CA

New China Buffet, Watsonville, CA

Grant Rd Gas & Auto, 1220 Grant Rd., Mountain View, CA

a garage in South City   the maze at the top of Bernal

flock of parrots near Corona Heights   fire escape with small avocado plant

anchor in little star   dahlias   carved pumpkins

paper wigwam   one sheet Ray Charles forever stamps

Winooski
Dog
Snake
Powder
Tigris
Mission Creek
Yellow
Russian
Salmon
Ganges
Sweetwater
Los Angeles
Kicking Horse
Peace

for Colter Jacobsen

THE PRESENTATION OF SELF
IN EVERYDAY LIFE

To choose not to
pick up phone & scroll anyway through
Dear old dreary daylit world, dull
·repetition of daily news, look up instead to see
a world newly cathected, autochthonous in
clouds, in ones and threes. All flux then only as
head? One sings to oneself & dreams—admiring
the birds: pigeons, a huge flock of them
alight & wheel—shoulder height gliding
through startled city humans already dazed
by afternoon light. Binary, octal
& hexidecimal numbers. The humor of being

reincarnated a lama, then identified as such
by selecting the attachments of a previous
ego. One sings to oneself momentarily
in words—decisive dilatory flight
concrete through concrete
canyons. Left like the lice on
Basho's robe. Your next episode playing
in sixteen seconds

LEVON HELM

A sunlight glints the head sees
A correspondent breeze
In the spittle & maw of the outside world
it wards away from, in order to form,
    & curls off below
Nascent again at passing by
sites of its earlier lives. Listening hard
& keen at all wrongnesses, never in
slumber but always an incidence
Evokes
Medium drive, starfish
        souvenir conjuring Florida's tall keys, with
        the weight things gifted obtain: on
looking back, a certain heft
Hard throwing away (precipice)
Books—anything lifted or on loan from
the libraries of friends & the voice / drum
    the inside the head is. Heavy
accumulation of definite articles. Spring!
    & Ill
Seen Ill Said beside My Life
& Happily. I'll weed. Small city garden—
Hortulan ataraxy of salvia & sage. By the
    window, a row of brightly
(different) colored
nail polishes. I wonder will "a sunlight the head
sees" seem or sound
        farther washed or faroff, hazy as the coast
        of New York across the wide summer glare

of Lake Champlain, green VT black flies & steam?
When I reread Nohow On or Writing is an Aid
       to Memory some day
next summer? The next? Ghosts. It's been spring now
off & on awhile, though in California the characters
of the seasons seem more muted. Kore following
the faintness of a lute through dry parking lots
stained with old oil. In my head dance the inhabitants
of a mysterious palace: pilgrims, messengers—
panting on perhaps toward
                      transfiguration—

as Malone, old sleuth, dying, tells
stories. Lies
flat on his back, like one of Chaucer's
                      ones: un-
accompanied now however—likewise unable
to shut up. Lone pilgrim going nowhere, delivering
       nothing
stripped of the canter not quite buried yet
either. Still keeps time
& sings: death chants, waltzes
hammers & circles. Familiar standards
by flickering light. Metal & country,
so fuck y'all. Ah the old nightmare
Reprise sepulchral perfection
eg. whichever way I fly I myself am etc.
All the old Lear lines behind Tears of Rage
Surface tension draws as majesty's cease—

a gulf
that draws me also nigh: but I'd wanted to breathe it all in

Early April air
with its undertones of frost & roots, pale pink
late afternoons again as (with small words)
a girl next door plays a game with her friends
cheering & yelling around a neighboring small city garden.
A firetruck's siren races by, loudly bending a bent
note. The only option today is everything—
a garden full of plants only whose names I know some of
        to weed. Although
observation impedes function in Stevens'
Description Without Place, & I'm compelled
to interrupt our conversation, despite not
having seen one another in so long, having so much to say
to Google ELONGATED SKULL PAINTING
still this very moment I am capable of just a little bit
of focused attention, modicum of capacity
concentration long enough to listen close
        in the wake of a motor, racing
waiting to find (I have to tell you) initial hum
        or rhythm, some
reliable rotation whatever so-called sense
might steadily arrange
                itself against: it gets me
                levitated, aloft in some
        otherworld—

A hummingbird in a canyon
Gone in sections
Misshapen in the head & at

Sunset a Joshua tree
Wrong at all incidence
Very far away now
In the drummer's head
As he sings
Pain, reliable through-line
What other song is there
Its repetition the head
Anchor wheel spiral
It's easy on roseapple island
You just try trying
To get to silence out of thin air
Since that's simpler than total noise
At least as long as one keeps breathing
If you're really listening a little bit
Of noise is all there ever is

Silver moon cigar box taped to the top of the snare
My mind already elsewhere

Enfranchised, at large, bold & unlit
A remnant of afternoon's shape taking on the character of flesh
before being hauled back beneath bladed starlight
raw teenage disturbance—a genre: the western fear again as in
Lear, of

nothing—black
engineer's boots, switchblades, greased down hair
Rand's Nietzsche rather than Gaddis', say—a hideous
   misreading
      the result of which

this polluted world in its apparent doxa, deal, or way—
      is. Although he
who wished to write & wring out play, whose
reveries then became the deepness of the pool: remains
political / apolitical
tender teenage trash. Pretty flowering weed in spring

I also like time-travel
I also like wailing on the traps with no invocation
alongside these ghosts whose senses guide me
Tidal as a third eye, conniving with
sublunary sets, in situ dragging
earth's seas. To teach them to sing
Amazing Grace shape note style, he sat
bolt upright in his coffin. To be handed
or (same thing) awaken
abruptly
      from it—since everything at least is
a double. Annie Clark runs into a rattlesnake naked:
& following the powerlines back to the road,
a rabbit ghosts the notion of kings. Selfhood—
a melody. Indra's net as the means of continually
making it. None of us
      ever thought to write a song

about all the shit that was going on
back then: war, civil war, revolution,
turmoil. Our songs were trying
to take you somewhere
else. I have
            minds in my head—

an amused oarsman, the moon
 a glimmering
cluster as it separates

        & reforms around
the dripping blade
of the oar. Clustered
            in separating

    important absent ideas
            rippling, starting to form
 a reflection:

        to get to
            'the point'
        is precisely
                the danger.

eg. Do away with the lead singer
No such thing as sidemen either
Yes an internal echo of the imperfect sound
Tough with knotty glissandos & clipped bits
of lifted (live) speech, now

gone. One obvious emblem—
the hummingbird I saw first thing on opening
the door this morning—patiently operating
through the apparent springtime
through the dependent deal
Of bougainvilla, lavender & sage. Through
weeds. Honeying neatly from each

& turning words' clusters
specific in specie tending toward unseen
suns, reaching
so as to reproduce
via pollination
Poets, that keep time & sing
so sing if you can
the numerous
Each one circulating
curling like that wake between landmarks—white
& seen far off in the bay: proof something's moving
that's the courtship
that's the approach
a foggy spring of weeds itself
cool & wet
as the underside of a pile of clouds moving
pretty gray anvil makes of the head
a marine layer, seeming
in some greater seeming—set in
nothing. A box the wind blown by
the mind, container ship out there

where Holbein's ambassadors now reappear
in all their goofy grandeur, silly worldly wealth
Heavy load beneath which
a horrible death's head in artful elongation & distortion gruesomely

yawns
at this crazed dying storyteller
this pilgrim going nowhere delivering nothing
this boy who hearing owls hoot, hoots back in wild
mimic rhyme—wild Arkansas farm kid
the drummer who sings & then so quiet in reverence
at the echoing from tall cliffs—memory & theft
& whose living eye, tender as an embryo, attends
the whiteness of the wake & attendant
waves: the mind
          piloting & piloted in by
                    "the mess," illustrious
nothing nothing names: a wave or wake as it
turns in on itself. Emptiness
in a technical sense. You hear it so clear
in Rick's voice, doing It Makes No
Difference: there's no escaping
this life with its owls rattlesnakes nectarines & kids
heartbreak red wine & malady, the early way
the sun slants in on the bed like an ancient tongue
mornings. No alternative to the next
moment: a negative connection & razor
sweet as jasmine. Non-duality is
why it makes sense to address the poem's readers

as travelers or lovers. Why my mind
weeding abandoned operates still through
this open book whose paragraphs are packed

with the names of people & places—
Sonny Burgess & the Pacers, Alberta, Duck Dunn
    & Lulu Reed
Roy Orbison, Memphis, Garth, Beethoven
& U.S. Grant. The redness of these cherries
has a particular dark red taste, as I spit
the pits back into the almost empty bowl. It's true
proper names are often used (as the philosophers
say) without "a fixed meaning"
except in the case you're looking directly—
as poets often are—at what you name. Thought, too,

        elongates
  as it picks up speed toward
  its unknowable
  vanishing points.

As spit inches toward a drain
or light to a black hole

    thought
      lengthens

                              seems to slide
                  slowly, then suddenly
                              sidelong

toward margin / cusp. Name. What this
bit chipped off in brilliance

whizzes toward—stands still or pivots on its
almost invisible wings. I had thought to send you

a letter. It became a corruscating dance held
minutely through the not-quite material world

of nectar & all the other aromatic colorful stuff
whose signature is disappearing everywhere

PROVIDENCE

A message about a lost bag of weed, a call from Mike Watt to Thurston Moore, taped full of static on an answering machine & recorded before crumbling piano chords on blown-out speakers: "call later—bye." You have to figure it was left on his machine during the making of Daydream Nation. It sounds simultaneously wistful & post-apocalyptic, as if nostalgic for something yet to happen. Falling right in the middle of an album this epic, some nostalgia for a sound, a high, distortion, the prefix "post-" on the most general level. & even as Daydream Nation contains it, "Providence" somehow manages to contain, or be the germ of, the lunge of this massive album in its entirety. When I arrive at any large body of work—Sonic Youth or whatever—I've learned I learn best by working at the edges. Now before I read Poe's "Murders at the Rue Morgue" I'll read his short essay "A Few Words on Secret Writing." It's the minor movements of these leviathans I'm obsessed with. That these dimmer passageways in works of art—God's foot on the treadle of the loom (Pip's dream in Moby Dick) ; or the couple of parts in Heart of Darkness where Conrad hurls us back to the boat on the Thames—all are parts that in reverse seem to summarize the whole. Contain it like a seed. I would like to read through completists' libraries like a magpie, picking up beautiful unmoored pieces of writing that might serve as metonyms for whole bodies of work. The resulting nest would probably be architecturally unsound but it would look good. In Spurs Derrida argues a fragment out of one of Nietzsche's notebooks—"I have forgotten my umbrella"—is a summation of all of that philosopher's thought.

All of which is tempting. On a less reductive level, it has always been precisely ephemera which remains, for me, unforgettable. What haunts me (& maybe "Providence," too) is an oblivion of memory; that the loss of the bits might prefigure a larger loss. By taping this message & making for it a memorial of decimated piano chords, tape-hiss & distortion; by putting it right in the middle of the album, the music recognizes that. Memory is an oblivion in which only ephemera floats to the surface. "You gotta watch the mota Thurston your fuckin memory is goin out the window." And dimmer passageways of large works of art, the moments that seem most resistantly minor, often epitomize the whole they inhabit for that very reason: the moments constitutive of any long process tether the "finished work" to the real, they're particulate matter. An answering machine message in the middle of Daydream Nation, like the apocryphal story about the lines Beckett typed into Ulysses, taking dictation from Joyce as he answered the door, may ring truest in large imaginative works because they are indeed true. Like newspaper glued to a painted canvas, which catches the eye & then the eye remains there, recognizing a likeness.

CITY BREEZE

Later, these things left littered
Seen as what ought have been caught
Little red & brown leaves scattered under
    living trees
Browns & greens. Sportive sure in lines
Lives. What one would see
Slowness of peeling the eye across
as plow or crow on ground or sky
        —pulled, wheeling—
 A search for only what is there—particular,
                present
    in only the slightest
        exactly what begins

To crumble, fall apart
In marble or in dew—to hew, little lights
Carved & seen singly or else fluent in
Sets: a trap one awakens
    as though "from," lets
Cool air dispelled over
(as fog rolls thickly in)
A bridge as of thought in reverse: how was it
for instance a bridge occurred?
    A sending set in what conceals
    To remain deadset on the hidden

Clasped in the mind as though it were a made thing
the mind's clasp suddenly shown in contortion
        the captive eye a little smoke
        on a horizon that holds it

All across lapses   the refrain forms   almost alluvial fan

All invention   simply stopgap   against breaking stride

Grains & bits   of things seen   solidly   only as

   In past or out

          terraced weakly in word space,
the impulse toward occular advantage instills its
imaginary code words, & breaks with actual
dawn. The real clouds (outside) pattern themselves
ignorant of but including the eye. Sound sets ears
forth, insinuating themselves into rain on the pavement,
a sequence from Ives. The open set (a series) of notes
is felt, a weirdly inward positioning. Dung beetles
navigate via the Milky Way. The body, apportioning
its bulk through city breeze, in fact operates as
canyon. Sunk into it are the air's feel & grit, smells—
rained-on jasmine, shit & gunk: tranched in unseen levels

   ten hours
   eleven steals

One is of a ground
evenly breathing unaware
The yellow crocus a spring snowbank
   suddenly includes

SAY

"what follows a strict chronology has no memory"
—Lyn Hejinian

There is no solitude. From now on
to witness

        stay
        a kid

    confidently repeating
                    the lip that got you slapped

      only because it was true

& steaming maintain (out-
                side
                    still) the capacity
                    to house

            a summer rainstorm

        stay

      a kid

      of crickets & lightning

MISSING HEAD

Pinned butterfly, salted
frozen fruit making meaning
things more mere "provisions"
& readier to be thrown away
Lazy as an afternoon spent
stripping copper wiring out
of sheetrock in an unfinished
subdivision, slowly separating
power cables, plates of
California light, "the turning"
names multiple concepts—in
sight but also a more deadly
"enframing," forgottenness
or coming-to-pass of
oblivion. The basis for
my taste in music died
homeless outside Boulder.
I'll read you one of the fragments
he wrote drunk on beam one night
in a beach-side town south of here:
Maybe I have cat scratch fever
Or maybe "fuego en mi casa"
The Spanish did not conquer me
Like the last time I looked
For cities of gold. Or that
Silly fountain that would make me
Endure. Sometimes I cannot
Believe the sun comes up
Does it know something I don't?

Between A's games & high lifes
he & I would work on these
pieces of the puzzle. "Thrown-ness"
however he never understood as
separate from "The Leap."
I wonder if he had any cigarettes
on him by the trailhead, & how
cold it would've been that time of year
in Colorado. Aristotle called
poetry "improper language" but he also
seemed wrong in believing there is
a "ground zero" for philosophical
thought. I'm sorry. & I agree
with you, too, as the days go by
anger is more the way I feel
than anything else. As fucked
as it sounds it is true that the best
of him was gone years ago. I stopped
looking for a logical explanation
lemonade in one hand
beer in the other. Go slow, sun
go slow. There's no disquiet
that one cloud could uncover
strapped by sunlight to a
plaid couch on the porch
watching a day like today
speak its giant language through
the disappearance of the only
cloud for miles. Strangeness

is a site where Being shows up
& this is exactly what's uncanny
or "unhomely" about us (as
humans). To shepherd the truth into
its house (the poem) & not instead
challenge it forth as a pitifully useful
tool of itself. & when I think
he was one of the smartest &
funniest humans the human parts
(generosity, openness, responsibility)
though they were at capacity
he never trusted in others enough
to get them up & running. Here's one
more I found in the past two months
it's called "FUCK YOU" & it goes:
I write because I am awake and moss
green, and it's raining outside—
minivans and orange sweatshirts
a green-eyed cat that
wants me as a master
or maybe a give-take relationship
gone now or is that the
minivan, no it's the cat
That's the whole fragment. Experts
say drug addicts & others including
jobless electricians & plumbers
are finding that copper & other
metals are relatively easy to steal
& sell to junk dealers who are largely

unregulated. For those seeking a quick buck,
there is nothing quite like metal. It is
91 degrees I read in Boulder today.
Mostly cloudy with wind coming in
from the west. The forecast is for
thunderstorms Wednesday Thursday
& Friday, clearing & sunny Saturday.
Speaking is hearing X. We
humans are reminded of it whenever
we open our mouths: not any ghost
in the machine type shit—the last
summer I had was in October
drenched in sun & beer. Now there's
no sweat still noir to line up as little agons
Mortals...needed & used for the
speaking of language

27.VI.12
QJC

SOME WATER

One word set forth, from it flow some more. "Water." You read water, or it is written down (phases of one activity). Following white whirls, the river branches out, instant digression. A bend of next association made, via sound, sense, or other means: wheel, say, or liquid. What is known about liquid? Liquid is relatively scarce. Scarce, that is, in relation to what humans know, to the known, to space-time. Wherever we are. We don't know if alien squid race through the freezing depths of the methane lakes that pock the surface of Titan, as it wheels Saturn.

In the scheme of things (ie., the physical universe we presently seem to inhabit) liquid is an exceedingly rare form for matter to take; it almost never happens. Here on earth we take liquidity for granted. Strange irony: the most common form matter takes on earth—liquid—is the rarest in the universe; whereas the most common form matter takes on the grand scale (the known)—plasma—is the rarest here at home. Solid and gas, nearly as familiar to us as liquid, trail behind, liquid being (of these three cosmological outliers) by far the most scarce. The saliva in your mouth is a gold ring on the beach.

Our bodies, all fat bone teeth and tongue, rest exquisitely precariously between states. Moment to moment we partake of all the forms matter does but as everyone knows the human body is mostly made up of water. At birth we are composed of about 78% water. Our liquidity positions us between the other two we're most at home with, gas and solid. Being human—being per se—seems to flow among these three familiar states of matter, and to grope wildly toward the mysterious fourth, plasma, of which lightning is composed. One thought (chain lightning) poets could hand off to ontologists would be to begin at thinking Being as precisely the straddling of these states, as a duration over time composed of the transversal, alternation, or alchemical transmutation between solid, liquid, and gas. Hilarious, humiliating, all-engrossing, sexy. Our form in Being (being) bends beneath the known, a slapstick process of matter encountering its various phases. Transversal being cleaves the distinctions, subtle and ambiguous, painful and pleasurable; at other times (in extremis of dithyramb, trance, or ekstasis) it annhilates them entirely.

So one begins like one of Beckett's protagonists, elemental, crawling through the mud, crashing through underbrush, pausing at the shore to stare out at sea, nowhere to go. Investigation at the most rudimentary level. Our simple grasp of the three most common forms matter takes turns into a comedy routine, or is shaded into primal nightmare. As Ishamel is magnetically drawn to water, so *Moby-Dick* begins; Truffaut's "The 400 Blows" freeze-frames Antoine's face after he runs out onto the beach and stops: the end. Plasma, the fourth phase, escapes us—we don't think as often *of* it but we may think *in* it, in flares and bursts of electricity. We will return to it, or it will return to us. Solids and gasses are familiar. Between ice and steam, the liquid state we call 'water' divides (unites) the two. Maybe it is because we have studied liquid fluidity—water—for so long that we call the four states of matter 'phases.' At the outbreak of western thought, the philosopher Thales stands staring out at the Aegean Sea from the shores of Miletus, formulating the idea of the arche as water. Although he disagreed with Thales Aristotle defended his reasoning, writing, "even the hot is created from the wet and lives by it."

We believe life requires liquid. But could the opposite be somehow equally true? Could belief formally mirror liquidity? Maybe liquid needs life and not just the other way around. Thales' notion of the arche stands at the start of western philosophy, and has as its source water: maybe thought attains to liquid form. In a solid state, the given molecules matter is made of are uniform and fixed; in gaseous form, they're diverse, unbound. As plasma, matter's molecules are hyper-charged, free-flying. Here on earth, matter tends toward the dynamic middle state: oceans, rivers, and thought are all said to flow. Heraclitus formulated the mind as a river, and the Greek root rheo carries the movement of water into our notion of rhetoric. Francis Ponge writes that water "collapses ceaselessly, at every moment renouncing all form." Thinking, then, may be a phase nouns pass through on their way to becoming ineffable. The mind as it reads / writes can occasionally feel as fresh, soluble and familiar as water. Thought, carried in mind, seems to slosh the rim of the bowl as does the Pacific against the rock it slowly erodes.

What would it mean for life to be the condition of possibility for liquid? (As Townes says, for the sake of the song, in its urge for paradox, erosion and reversal.) The idea that language springs into being as a response to the (melting) consciousness which considers it. And that mind finds correspondent form in the most likely form it sees: liquid. A mind grappling in the dark for correspondences makes of itself a river, in metaphor.

It carves (craves) the noise and solidity of obdurate mind, erodes the hardened shoals and heavy banks of instrumentalized rationality. Logic is piers thrust into an ocean, and its erosion proves it always already at least half submerged. Poets are students of liquidity that then theorize the plasma state, and regard it with fear, noise, awe, love—poetry. It is the big howling void at which we throw old songs. Water is our familiar teacher (language) and our mother. Water matters like thought, pooling language into the depths of unanswerable questions. Meaning's a matter of mattering, slow accretion of materials. Language (if not meaning) flows inevitably, finding its level, even when the speaker wishes to dam it up or alter its flow.

The Yogacara (mind-only) school of buddhism views a storehouse of underlying mind as an ocean of consciousness, with seven types of thought skimming its surface as waves. Consciousness still as deep ocean, pitch dark maybe at the Mariana Trench like depths, then roiled with surface action, wind blown, active and colored every way the light (all other phenomena) catch it. Viktor Schauberger speaks of water's ability to hold emotion, or valences of thought and feeling. Thoreau and many others speak of time as a stream.

Vico, in his verum factum principle, defines the knowable—even that which might be known at the most distant (spooky action) remove—as the made. From the earliest cave paintings, dreaming handprints on red walls, through film reels in dark theaters, what constitutes the known only grows. It unrolls, multiplies, widens and deepens. Crackling with energetic potential it gropes chaotically toward a radically free, ionized state which, plasma-like, seems both to outpace and anticipate human knowledge.

Plasma makes up stars and the space between them. Theorizing matter's phases, our neurons fire, and the terminals of dendrites form in the massively coiled mysterious far-off adjacent neighborhoods of the human brain. Do the electrical impulses the human brain creates form flashes of plasma matter? If matter finds its most familiar cosmological form there, that's when it would—in thinking. Think thinking plasma, language liquid. Rare clear and (for us) familiar flow in a wild expanding known. Taste your lips, and think it, speak.

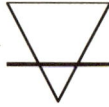

North a drum heaved storm out of salt, cave set (as diamond) in depth of forest. Fury of dogs and horses breaking branches, little jade light thrown down through pentacle, a nurse's touch. Cool dry timber line, perimeter drawn down into tight knot bound by weight of coal—compressed vegetation turned firedamp black, magnetized. That specific old lightness, a sheaf of wheat ore cut to alternate—once in the ground to rot back on, forgive and moss. All low things touch. With mole knowledge, in worm length below wild green the cows ruminate and muddy in brown streams. A hold in berm, series of sets. Steaming, its surface at spring dawn. Banked in brambles out which branch a flowering wand. Cups of dark wine, small bright copse of verdant bed envined. Where couples couple. A graphite sulfur and gold meridian slag of horizon in serpentine and talc, Diodorus' extreme azimuths first root organ from quartz, in vetiver rhizome is henge calligraphy. Fossilized radicle set forth in petrified form, whose iron's reflected in red Mars. From oceanic garnet out via time to blown dune spores still lean in on the wind, grow ghostly under moonlit hardened burgundy pitch. An elementary music with four quarters of frigidity slowly composes itself. Out striation of jet flock cornflower & vetiver, rock formation in time is firmament process. It grounds living in the negative charge of oxidation, reduction, trash / health, all matter marsh to single leaf rotting into mud, each mote of dust as Mater.

The negative charge, chthonic, a stable cold dryness ancient people perceived. In the electrical current of myth an ion is grounded, reversed; embodied in Demeter, the work (myth, poem) is then *in* it. Neither is without the other. Serpentine formed at great depth then occurs millennia later, glittering jade on forest floor. What shelters rootstock, in carbon and silica, giving way to systems completely alien to the crystal's, expressed instead in stamen and leaf. A sheltering giving forth what is wholly its other. Molten fragments cooled and scattered, stack and slag, little hills of coarse grain. Batholith to country rock to palmful of dirt, hyle whose rocklike systems are bent folded entrenched into our oldest stories. Hecate Swamp Thing and Geb. Salt circle dissolved into ammonite and moss in reverse. Spiral jetty resurfaces in autumn sun a pomegranate tree, sea of sap and salt. Doorways to the glittering, dripping world—at lava river, or Carlsbad, in the iron that reddens one's gums. Cobalt copper and phosphorous of gut and eye in open mine, or in calcium carbonate dripping over millions of nights to form columnar limestone jewels in caves. The thingly character our words are in: what changes, layers, ignites them. That out of it they might form something soluble, change into a green chute that lived and died. The bed stays, shelter and grave. Dreaming nurse howling packs of wolves run across, the warm rock face snakes sun themselves upon, what swallows all rain in field, in block and plate.

Slow moving solution or slag which dandelions pure arrest of time, yellow to gray out of tourmaline, and crumble, drift. So on having crossed it, the lintel's always strangely beneath one's head, or is their future bed. Under mountain great pile of rocks shift in sleep. The dogs move in restless pack length of valley floor horses' bones become. Leaves what mud the horses' hooves have and will beat into shape. Horizon of are, at all times in slow cataract under. The health of the heap, dark warm heart in low beats, what sends forth chutes that breathe thin air above. All light leaves hidden. Cool wet hugely slabbed and veined mass, a meld of the vertical held slowly in place, the unseen work a complete mixture cooling. A weather record faded into mellow bloom, lichen kaleidoscope eating granite folded out of sediment, red green meteorite seer. Loam of tertiary to sequence and range. Sheared serpentine juniper holds and feeds from, bent out of green billion old heart. Slow half-silent burrowing music, a form of black below pendant moss, in hollow carved out beneath limestone overhang, water first issues—spring out of shale silt and alluvial debris.

As climb to wood out of steeping tea, smoke stained and begun. The high dry entisols, gold sand hills. A chart plain visible of accreted millenia, in iron vine moss and root. What steadies the rhizome lightless and heavy, situating everything green. The held firmament blends a series—immovable immovably springs forth all that leaps and uncurls toward air and the sun. An iris opens above. Dogs in Pleistocene packs on over through dim blue space worn stone. An extension through humus and lichen beneath decomposing leaves deepening into striations of jade. Dripped into dug and carved out of invisible rivers into cathedral, backward spire, initially maze—what ancient poets said water changes into before finally taking form. What unthought tons of dark displaced for an ounce of gold they later carried, held. Cinnamon-colored beetles, death's heads, worms moles centipedes home in blocks and slabs, ice's thawing forms in pulp of swamp that push out cattails, marsh, reeds and fern as marble snakes through clay. Mounded around canals at rills rings and hollows, pumice sulfur salt and coal. Down among the possibility, in the seeds of things, in spores of fungi hardness and glint soften and dim into the every that, having grown out of it, die back in. Under deep frost or trackless sand blown into hot razors lie sleepless tint of bursting green, a chartreuse the beloved's eye was born to see. Burbling in gorges or traced out in hazy ridgelines—

Hidden rhizome rootbender old quartz in mud, dustless gleaming mirror in ground: strength of granite in its mammoth seams, the history of all interglacial weather, heat and wet rendered cool, hard, drying to dust. The softening slowness of time rendered graywacke and diamond, a pile of shifting sands under sun. Dirt soil aggregate wormshit compost decomposes nouns into verbs—and back again, sends forth a daisy to slurp down rain into itself and turn to face the blazing sun. All that roots big rumbling quiet slabs and blocks, that dreams mountains into place. What ferns and nasturtiums fan, grace—dripping green jewels, moss hung off a stone, rich black antonym of abstraction. Spoke a word of origin, its initial dark cool substance always different, and to manifest something wholly other. Never for it, but (indirectly) by virtue of each. This palmful black and granular, that dry full yellowy dust all common to the living become visible. Left at a loss with matter, in repose and response it sets grass into growth and slowly forests itself, holding quiet dark against endless surge of sea and lightening world, lambent air. Holy unholy core coal black skin a glacis of leaves unfolding into stem and vein. Teeth a stone, a series of peaks, a rock ranging its spine south into ocean. Rock dust piled into crystal heaps a system as of living eyes, particle hidden eyes alive to amethyst gleaming in dark chambers. Clouds expanding out into fissures and tunnels, an array.

Condensed dependent metals, thickly ranged in low sets, mineral subject of heart and rock's cold substrates, where thought slowed to bare incidence allows only hints of far-off weather. Other under every out forth, what the if must split or situate its notion in the dark density, the composite of. The *of* in 'of all' as wholly mixed—wolframite, iron, lazurite and zinc. In an uneven slab, running through coarse grain north to cold dirt interval, only then opening out into sluice or fan—mud miasma substrate mixture mess.

What any all must first give forth from out: cold low northern issuant, that he'd fein be a tracklayer somewhere in the orbit of. What priests sprang forth from, the dream layer. A bed of iron, salt and quartz, belted—hung in golden leaves and led out through in clear spigots. Fold after mineral fold, held. A form light over time might take at depth. Gesture's opposite. Weathered pedalfer drummer silt in dream of glacial drift. A series occuring under tall fibrous grasses, beneath Venus and the Moon. Endeavor's basis. The lag or plinth at which all marvel, infant, takes hold and nurses. Thinking's catch, unhurried to near-complete stasis. In channers and cobble of sand, silt and clay, any composite in which root might take hold—from hardpan below hummock out to glacial till over granite and schist. Dry turning cold. Amid the bright hard weather record break down forms that also breathed. Leaves, radiolaria, rats' skulls, the nearly translucent shells of snails—what held light or worked it, at pains and with bliss through cells. Tanbark twigs, purple clover, the seeds of figs rot amid agate obsidian and pitch. Among emeralds and sapphire. The shells tissues and nails of things bloom into morel, into bear's head tooth and white chantrelles before decaying back into dirt. Heavy slow lucid opener changes millenial registers. A crush—tectonic, glacial—of names toward lucent green chute the thread: a verb. Devotion devotion devotion. Core hid, skin held dry to cool off a history of the rates of change. Since it is fall one lets oneself be led. To think of it as a store is the grave misperception: look, it holds. Permanent movement of the almost-stasis.

WIRE

diamond, pyramid
   skull & shovel

S   H   A   D   O   W   S

An obligation to the imaginary world
from which I make my departure

Something important about
the self & the other

a remark a philosopher made
which when you look for

the exact quotation, isn't
there. Is different. Always
     check out

reflections in water—a string
of orange flags appears

    in the water
       by the pool

"Beauty is so rare a thing."
An obligation to

the imaginary world
an approach to dreaming: a sail

on the horizon becomes
a smear of paint. Shadows,
    like water, exhibit

surface tension,
bend & attract. We are

in this looking
& late to learn what's what

Life's an illusion. But you don't
hear much about that these days.
    The wire on which

birds shuffle, over which
planes rumble into view

runs thru ever present over
head the head sees:

equally veiled
in their logic,

the oneiric
& the haptic. Did you

hear what I said?
Have you lived here long—

"Beauty is so rare a thing"

To speak of music, of so much
     flowery earth. "What
     do you do?"

                             "I work
receiving. Nights, mainly, & early
mornings. It's quiet, & I can read
in the stockroom. I always
bring a book."

MODIFICATION OF CLOUDS

Crepuscular
tough glissando
syntactic structures
sutured into stacks

    heliosheath
    autocorrect
    textless adspace
    reformat mute
      voyager

ie., someone had gills

Science, sad cyclops
After having invented
    the Cosmos
Attempted to shackle
    the enigma—

clouds in loosely pulled
chunks let go
plus mud among
fresh cut grass
then what I think of as
my long-forgotten
    problem

    a baffling silence
    between these discrete

noises
displays my mind
to me

Lightly agitated
as a tree

ANAPOLOGETOS

"An eye as a car that it's in"
—Clark Coolidge

Inferring the presence of people
From an airplane window

The easy roads, clover-
leafs & refineries
The history of Neanderthal DNA

& more broadly, the rectangular
Wheeled metal snack & drink cart

Pushed through light tilted around
The aisle & surrounding cabin

Of air as to wooded lots & neatly
Ordered cul-de-sacs

A repetition of development
Mirrored aloft by wheels, wings
& black smoke

FLITCRAFT

The Flitcraft thing is positioned almost midway through Dashiell Hammett's *Maltese Falcon*. If you are unfamiliar with it, it is well worth checking out the entire novel even just for this anecdote, which is both incidental and integral to its host. I won't summarize the plot of the parable here, I would rather try and express the enormity of my interest in it, and maybe even articulate a reason for that interest. Stemming, I suspect, from my devotion to poetry, I love the Flitcraft story the way taggers love post offices. I'm in good company, too—the Mekons tip their hat to this mystery man on "Fear & Whiskey," one of their finest records. I think the Flitcraft episode fascinates us as a device that scotches the process of the book in which it appears, becoming thereby (weirdly) even more necessary to that larger framework. It's like a flickering hologram, or a kernel panic. The story persists in the novel's world as a very particular point of departure. It's a static on the band that can't quite be squelched, a marker where the choice to do the reverse was made.

Flitcraft, we're told, "felt like somebody had taken the lid off life and let him look at the works," precisely at the moment when Hammett does the same thing. In channeling this story through Sam Spade, he raises the shutter of the novel, exposing its filaments. Right where they break. Fatal error is the parable's allure: it's a set piece precluding the very notion of motive in the mystery in which it's been lodged. Spade casually tosses the story off, but the fact it is casually tossed off is firmly established. It's an intentional glitch.

I put this short writing about Flitcraft here to surround it with left-overs. Film leader, microphone wire, canvas stretchers. The workers building the sound stage are on lunch break, and the orchestra is tuning up. It sounds like noise; it is noise. Maybe these are circumstances which will result in something like the Bent Pyramid or the Tacoma Narrows Bridge. An interesting collapse in a world where beams do or don't fall. Any and every Either / Or world. A collapse taking the form of a digression.

The point isn't that we return to a world very different from the one we left, or (more uncomfortably) that it's somewhat similar on return. Although it's tempting to focus on the difference. The realization that one's departure can be complete, and that this departure might be incidental to the world—that it might take the form of an anecdote within the story, a slight branching out—belies the difference between the world one departs and the world one is (just as arbitrarily) returned to. Whether you step out of your life into a Constable cloud study or "The Man who Shot Liberty Valence;" into Grampus or Sleep; into Monk doing "Easy Street," it is the absoluteness of the departure, and its sidebar relationship to continuing reality, which reveal the oblivion in which any "larger plot" already rests, and from which, as from a dream, it emerges. The oblivion into which you and the song, the painting, the book, are swallowed whole. It is from that dream these failures, trailing their blue tape and stencils, reliant on darkrooms and static—momentarily—deliver us. "Like a fist when you open your hand."

HUMAN-IN-THE-LOOP

Quilt
in bass drum, a mistake you pay
        increasing attention to
Put dimmer switch
on shade of tree
This is the perfect thing to do
Warm winter yellows
Scotch the process
Heave dampener
& then snap tight
        as a jewel case
thinly erupt into
squiggly lines, something
you can associate
        to
Calmly loading the boat w/ notes
One familiarizes the composition
        with
Over-the-shoulder
(that's not quite right)
focus
to get out of
the jam of
describing

                        27 IX 12

A DETOUR

With My Back to the World

& intonation sufficiently ambiguous

All my merit spoken for, earmarked—to allow the neutral valence,
   a necessary precondition

As electrical contrivance, a means of strange underwater conveyance

So nice I cried in the aquarium shop

All my merit D.O.A., all my merit already done for

MORE EMPTINESS

In which to bloom violently forth

To draw a murmur across

Twilit sky, in parochial evenings of late wind

Stevens: life without poetry as life "without sanction"

ie., Aeolian Harp / leaf-blower

That might also speak with a miraculous organ

Eating & handling money

Nothing survived the 20th century

Straight is the passageway which leads to sleep and a dull kind of
   faith in the odds

Lonely eyeball, whole integer sunk in pearl

On tapering wheel of mind

A prosthetic for the name

Vaping, gaming

Wound up stampeding one's head into mush

As far as the latest global frontier

Smashed cerebral interruption

It complicates itself, or we complicate what we consider it

Every exit builds another tunnel

The moon in the water lovely lively aware

As does dogs' ability to smell in stereo, which is why they of-
ten turn in circles

Horribly twisted, as an electrical cord

How many times eg., Brodey must've said, "tomorrow I'm
turning back to the poems," torching one last one as the sun
came up orange bloody & wrong

Rusted bicycle bones out by the manmade beach

Earthquake rubble plowed into a narrow sound

Unexpected pleasure, a detour on the way to the obstacle

Mike Tyson Punchout, ashtrays, Cosmo & Nightmare on Elm
Street

My four-wheeler education

Capacity to not quit (ever quit) writing in dumb log cabin
   appearance

Iggy & Florian, shopping for asparagus

"I just always feel rustic around those people"

Who broke their arm?

Can song be said to precede the metaphor?

Blake Shelton moondancing in cowboy boots

Zantac, Lexus, Arrowhead, Denali

Picasso: "a hoard of destructions"

Grand opening of a psychic's storefront

Always keeping to surface streets, moving nevertheless quick

Alive to the least familiar blocks

Invitation toward the infinite series each day is

Clotheslined by advertising & smoked

As Lopez loosens up in the pen

It's a real good time if you're not

Life doesn't seem like real life, so which is—it switches

The dog barking at the beginning of Fahey's "Poor Boy"

· The whorehouse in Peoria where Richard Pryor was born

Another appearance not to dismiss

In dogwood, in sweet maple & birch

The fresh health of a tree's new limbs

Longest relay race ever

EARTH   HEART
GRAVE   DIGGER

Aeneas at the prow of the boat, offering entrails to the salty
waves

Across from which is this image of it

Like almost like

Type "Dis" into Google you get Disney's stock info, no entry
on Hades

With these ghosts whose senses guide me, whose beliefs I re-
fute

To take mild description & then walk away from therein

Everything unaccounted-for: life

Free Alicia Keyes concert

Big & gauzy, set apart

In backyard of head, in head's meadows

That what is mysterious might further confound us

As the Trojan ships turn into girls—

Solid tacit free mysteries

Beckett: "The danger is in the neatness of identifications"

That it's Spicer's own violins that persecute him

SDS broke a lot of plate glass windows Vladimir & Estragon wound
up cleaning

Sabbath has a song about it. Time's in twain—night's at odds with
morning; our crepuscular poets argue it out

Who sees ghosts of the self's own invention

That the kid with the first person shooter on the bus turns up the
volume, lazily is killing the sun sprawling mid-aisle

Guarding the most precious & obvious things

In fluid moving squares

To level crime with a child's playthings, summer afternoon, dew-
points & crystallizing

Hejinian: "Unhappily, time seems more normative than place"

Toward strangeness as an in, the little love of being amid

Strange sunny sunday singing

Smallness as opposed to repeatability

Preparing a slight

Embassies for your concern

Precision of mid-day jet trail over causeway, idle haze: the
atrocity dotted in palms & high pinks

A real tricycle of conversation takes place, skill of the skull

As mid-convivial the cortex slides tongueward

Consider the physical principle of displacement

I'm getting there

Just before music

"The transformation is incomplete," said the cloud to the
hillside

What is it of answers any accident

ENDURANCE

Coded benedictions, these
letters between friends—
whatever green grows between
cracks (the accidents accreted called
"living" for which
we retain a keen taste) written in invisible
or disappearing ink. Thinking, never
thought
so-called "complete." Optimally passed fast

Along the regular route, following the progress
of certain construction jobs
I forget to smoke until I'm already in the lobby
or awaiting the train, its large codes

reciting Blake from memory
AGENT HAS NO MONEY

a tourist always on my own w you
then I disembark solo, w a loaded
endurance

& in the downtowns of cities
(I picture them fictionally, as
brains, the financial districts the
brain-damaged parts of a brain)
I invent my intentions as I go

until you're right there w me
& your letters, gifts—things

lifted or on loan, slightly more dilating
but at least as temporal
as this transfer which reads
GOOD FOR TRAVEL IN ANY DIRECTION

OWL

my advantage lies in knowing
even the beautiful are susceptible
to the human crisis, is it
ridiculous as me
welding my desire to your hair
save your pity
for those who do not
even have this
means of resistance
say nothing to nobody
speak nothing to anyone
never say nothing
to get better at it, is it better
to do it all of the time or never
& by never at all I mean constantly
thinking about it with a basic
static wariness changing
the locks (names)
then when I attempted feeling
hatred
telling anybody nothing
never saying anything to nobody
I told anybody anything

RAW UMBER

free of not free to
not wanting something for no
reason
remembering to take it easy
whatever the cost
oh honey you can fight two fronts
do it with marmalade
man-made vices made you
pale & nervous as a ghost
In rebelling against these
2 certain masters
you see how ugly they are
they hold down your neck with war
they never were real friends
So take it easy whatever
the cost. Get away & go
outside. Out
here's where there's not that
more the accidence of egality
Look: tiny orange
butterflies crown clover
bees inspect
every angle for
the nectar, their
little jewelers' lupes
eyeing clovers' coronas
starbursts
it is these animals to whom I owe
a debt of gratitude larger than poetry

ACTION CANNOT BE UNDONE

This

Outside the mind, like a great
monument abroad suddenly
come upon under construction:
immediately familiar behind
traffic, scaffolding & ladders.

Chi Ama Crede. The person
who is trying to kill you
            is yourself

10 IX 15 – 1 X 16

OF AND OR FROM

This morning a monk
on the 43 asked me
to pronounce & explain
the word 'eligible'—he'd written it
in Cambodian next to itself
in English on a yellow
legal pad, he had on blue blockers
with a line of palm trees the bus
windows reflected between glare
& coincident passengers—
friendly smile, thin mustache

Odds are the Big Bang happened
elsewhere and / or before however
we are

of and or from
it: where *of* has the sense to flow out from
                              some larger or
                              habitual whole

Saul *of* Tarsus, for example. Who of course
became Paul: he writes he knew a man
who was caught up in the third
        heaven, is that man

however, him? Are there though
larger & smaller wheels I asked
the monk who was interested in

eligibile & he said sure but
it's the same buddha.

In pursuit of my mess-making
        capacity

I'd like this eligibility
for every nearness to
what we're of
& possibly even
in waking life
        remain—

I realize my motion is
but is proved to be are: inside

a myriad of the minds
as though what I slough were of

RAIN

whyever I have to continue
insisting on myself & ought instead
remain scarce & diverse, rough
around the edges, my perimeter
bleeding into the landscape
surrounding me

& when I say the landscape
surrounding me I mean everything
which actually I am
rough around the edges with

As Creeley quoting I believe Olson
(I'm paraphrasing—actually all of this
is paraphrased, what movie or any art isn't
"based on a true story") put it We are
as we're finding out we are

getting off BART in the east bay
a profusion of bougainvillea. I jam my
hands in my pockets—the squelch of
static on the classical band & a shear
of afternoon light my perceptions

are razed in. To want something intensely
is valuable, & then to get it & give it away

WHAT WHEN

"I have no way & therefore want no eyes"

—Gloucester, *King Lear*

what is not
to move

        marked improvement
        making great strides

        It delights him to think of these
        thrust into the grime as he is

any don't no
what heel say   tilly does so

      obsolete sonar operating in long
      streaks of fate

      "so long, car"

to old-fashioned text
what when

      It delights him to think of these.
      The characters in his stories
      would relax w/ cigarettes & beer

pushing a sore leg along
rain, geese
form a Queequeg vee, tattoo it

as on sky over
jet cloud over

city

presently the figure
drew near, passed & proceeded

on its halting way

drawing near, the figure
passed & proceeded

having no need for
artillery dump, aorta—   the wrong time
                                  the clock on
                                  the bus keeps
                                  displaying

& some speed metal
to clatter the ambiguity

"in the knot of"

As vague hub on general wheel. All you meet is
wealthy landlords, pretzel-eaters & undertakers, other misshapen
        passers-by
mishappen

                        impossibly rare
                        peach on the beach, pure

fabrication of memory

        always going
        always never gone

THE DIFFICULTY

The difficulty
a series
of thoughts
falls
apart, as a
tower & now
one starts
from square
one is
an illusion
of course—
thought's not
(isn't) stacked that
neatly & square
One is always there

BETWEEN THE IDEA OF THE THING
& THE THING ITSELF

thin drizzle on the window, the wing's
shadow on the cloud
               thought it was a canyon
that crayon's my big idea, endearing myself to raw umber
    svaha

The length of slippery rail season depends
on fall weather conditions and the quirks
of Mother Nature. But until
the weather turns frosty
and all the leaves have fallen SEPTA

did I ask or did I
just get off the train & take it back
                   in the other direction
                   svaha
I once saw
lighting curled in a cloud, the cloud-fist
hidn't
the lightning, thin electric
       crackling twins

"folks, look out—the doors are loose"

this is Nassau, next stop Greenpoint
where I
       weirdly alight

ACKNOWLEDGMENTS

These poems initially appeared in various chapbooks and journals—

Spirits & Anchors (Auguste Press, 2010); *Local News* (Bird & Beckett, 2013); *Takes* (Bootstrap, 2015); *Late to Practice* (Dirty Swan Projects, 2017)

All I See is Re(a)d, Amerarcana, Big Bell, Boog City, Dreamboat, Elderly, Emerald Tablet, Greetings, The Life & Death of American Cities, Peacock Online Review, Sprung Formal, TRY!, The Tsatsawassans, Vitriol, Where Eagles Dare.

Thank you: Micah Ballard, Sunnylyn Thibodeaux, Julien Poirier, Evan Kennedy, Patrick James Dunagan, Ava Koohbor, David Brazil, Sara Larsen, Alan Bernheimer, Nicholas James Whittington, J Grabowski, Kevin Killian, Eric Clifford, Joseph Shelley, Derek Fenner, Ryan Coffey, Ruslana Lichtzier, John Coletti, Alli Warren & Colter Jacobsen.

Thanks & love to my family. For Sally my everyday thanks, immediate & bounded by the local, bigger than cities & stars. For the dance & all.